YABU PUSHELBERG

Dear Steve,

To a life of creative,
inspiration and wonder.
There is design by us and
collaborative art by others which
I'm sure you could appreciate.

#19/1.
George   x   [signature]
                Dec 21, 2009

First published in the United States of America by
Architecture/Interiors Press, Inc.
4455 Los Feliz Boulevard, Suite 106
Los Angeles, CA 90027
www.architectureinteriorspress.com

ISBN 978-0-9823190-0-0

Library of Congress Control Number: 2009925368

Printed in China
Design: HKcreative, Inc.
Rick Simner Design

YABU PUSHELBERG

WILLIAM NORWICH

EDITED BY CAROLYN HORWITZ AND ANTHONY IANNACCI

ARCHITECTURE/INTERIORS PRESS, INC

We dedicate this volume to our staff,
both past and present. While their process may not
be immediately apparent from the images here,
their love of a spectacular interior is. We thank them
for enthusiastically taking on each project
as if it were their first and last.
George & Glenn

THE HAZELTON HOTEL
TORONTO

8

TELL ME ABOUT MYSELF

"Tell me about myself," the elegant lady said, her enigmatic smile like kindling.

After visiting in her townhouse, getting to know each other, testing, checking, assessing, dancing ideas like beaux and sweethearts, these were the words, the direction and instruction, that sealed the commission that brought to Manhattan one of my favorite places, Carolina Herrera's flagship boutique on Madison Avenue. It's all about that double staircase to stylish heaven in Manhattan hell, all the promise, all that magic—designed by George Yabu and Glenn Pushelberg.

"Tell me about myself." Doesn't that sound luxurious? I can hear Mrs. Herrera saying it, supremely confident and self-knowing, needing no one to tell her about herself but welcoming the Yabu Pushelberg five-star treatment.

Of course she entrusted the project to Glenn and George. As Coco Chanel, her ancestor in the fashion firmament (related by talent and tradition, not blood), once said, "An interior is the natural projection of the soul." Souls had met, and matched. And the result, like all Yabu Pushelberg projects, is an environment of great feeling and stature. "Good architecture is iconic, but architectural interiors need to be emotional," Glenn says.

For their passion and their exquisite attention to detail, to locality, to both suitability and theatricality, to their narrative rather than conceptual approach to telling their clients' stories in magnificent interiors that evoke longevity, in a culture where style substitutes for substance—if Yabu Pushelberg didn't exist in the pantheon of current interior design, we'd have to invent them. "Design has to be about the invention of things," says George, "but people get confused with styling."

Personal as well as professional partners, George and Glenn met nearly 30 years ago at university in their native Canada and now keep offices in New York and Toronto, with a staff of about 100 working on projects from Moscow to Mumbai.

A series of big breaks, like waves, one after the other, buoying them around the world, began with designing the Club Monaco stores in Canada. They then moved on to great residential projects; hotel interiors including the St. Regis in San Francisco, the W in Times Square, the Four Seasons Tokyo, and the fabulous Hazelton in Toronto; shops for Bergdorf Goodman, Kate Spade, and Tiffany & Co. in New York; and Louis Vuitton VIP suites and Lane Crawford department stores in Beijing and Hong Kong, just to mention a few. Current commissions include working with Ian Schrager on a boutique hotel for his new Edition brand, renovations of Paris' Printemps department store, and a Park Hyatt hotel in New York.

The journey of Yabu and Pushelberg, this album, begins now. Welcome to the wonderland. What are you feeling in these rooms? Daydreaming? Sensation. Sound. Scent. What are your favorites? Where does your soul sit? Tell us about yourself.

CLASSIC LUXURY

For the rich, and for the not-so-rich, status is how much space you take up.

It can be a huge down parka or an excessively large and obstructive shoulder bag worn on a crowded city bus in Boston, or it can be a 7,000-square-foot McMansion on a small plot in Bridgehampton. The common thread is that at some point, at least in the marketing of the aforesaid, they have been described as "luxury" items.

"Luxury" is one of the most misshaped, misunderstood words in our current cultural vocabulary. It was never intended to be a synonym for demonstrably expensive; it was intended to describe an experience. But in music videos and weekly tabloid glossies, it is a high-flying catalogue of things most-wanted, ranging from "it" bags to speedy motorboats, magnums of champagne, caviar facial masks, and lots and lots of jewelry, the more golden and diamonded the better.

In interior design, luxury has become defined as forgetting about the edifying processes of things with spatial or constructional quality in favor of quicker satisfaction: blatant displays of easy-to-see expenditures like whirlpool baths, at-home spas, marble—any marble—laid any which way, faux finishes, and indoor and outdoor sound systems that scream "expensive" and may cause infertility in your neighbors.

Ah, but classic luxury, as practiced by the greats, is another story entirely. First of all, it is a story that barely whispers and never screeches or asks to be looked at.

Luxury is quiet. Luxury is time.

Friendly or service-oriented environments, rendered in high-quality, timeless materials or with a modern take on design classics, have charisma, but you will need the antennae to find it, to feel it, to trust it. There are some people who need years to understand this, and there are some who are born getting the gentle message. The distinction was drawn years back by Marella Agnelli (speaking of classic luxury) who told Sister Parish (speaking more of classic luxury) that so-and-so—no names, because it is luxurious to practice the quietude one preaches—"would take a generation to understand wicker" as she feathered a Fifth Avenue nest with hideously expensive antiques that would have made even old man Duveen blush. The nouveau riche woman in question, it seemed, was shopping faster than money could be minted. Acquiring all great pieces, yes, but with a swiftness of consumption that was not heartfelt, not the soft, harmonious medley of gracious notes occurring organically.

"Understanding true luxury, and being one of the people who knows where to find it, hidden in the details, rather than the obvious displays, needn't take long anymore. Because of travel and the media, the eye is educated very quickly nowadays," observes George. Adds Glenn: "Luxury is not only in the detail. It is also in having the time, or taking the time, to look for it, find it, and experience it."

Look over here, look over here.

MAIMON WINE & GRILL
TOKYO
16

LOUIS VUITTON VIP SUITES
HONG KONG

30

W HOTEL TIMES SQUARE
NEW YORK
36

THE HAZELTON HOTEL
TORONTO

FEAST FOR THE SENSES

"Architecture," Richard Neutra said, "is illuminated not only by the light but by the sound as well; in fact it is brought into relief for us through our senses."

However, what is a feast for the senses to some is famine to others. Kubla Khan did not his pleasuredome decree to everyone's taste—in fact, he'd probably never get the necessary permits to build nowadays, even in the splashy Hamptons. Mr. Morgan's Italian Renaissance-style library by Charles Follen McKim had its detractors, as did Catherine the Great's perfumed summer palace, where her lover Potemkin would come to her in her exquisite bathhouse (really the world's first residential gym), naked save for his open dressing gown and a pink bandana—but what shade of pink, was it hit or miss?—although historians are unclear where exactly said bandana was fixed.

Other critics of sensorial abundance: the many architects who have a mortal fear of color, so that everything has to be either black or white or some monochromatic compromise between the two ... How do you say beige in Beijing? (Yabu Pushelberg, it is happily reported, are not afraid: Consider as Exhibit A their Lane Crawford department stores.)

On the other hand, there goes Dorothy Draper exclaiming in decorator's heaven, "The drab age is over! Color is coming into its own again." Which will make some see red, and will remind others of Diana Vreeland's "Garden in Hell," which is how she described her Park Avenue apartment, her feast for the senses, where everything read red.

"All my life I've pursued the perfect red," she once said. "I can never get painters to mix it for me. It's exactly as if I'd said, 'I want Rococo with a spot of Gothic in it and a bit of Buddhist Temple'—they have no idea what I'm talking about. About the best red to copy is the color of a child's cap in any Renaissance portrait."

But try explaining this search for red bliss to the teenager sitting next to you on the family sectional, lost in the latest "Grand Theft Auto" video game. Mrs. Vreeland's sumptuous goals will not compute. He'll roll his eyes and ask you, please, not to assault his senses with such blather.

There is no right or wrong; life is a banquet for the senses, or it can be. But in order to communicate, modern design must reach these days to hold the attention of a culture both highly sensitized (the Vreelands, as it were) and desensitized (the teen lost in video land). Color, texture, sound, fragrance, technology, clever mixings and juxtapositions, state-of-the-art materials and sources reclaimed—all stimulate and revitalize the viewer.

"Concern with effect rather than meaning is a basic change of our electric time," observed Marshall McLuhan, "for effect involves the total situation, and not a single level of information movement."

With so much to accomplish in order to succeed these days, can design also be entertaining? "It *should* be entertaining," enthuses Glenn. "Entertaining, but not exaggeration." Meaning feast, not freak show, for the senses.

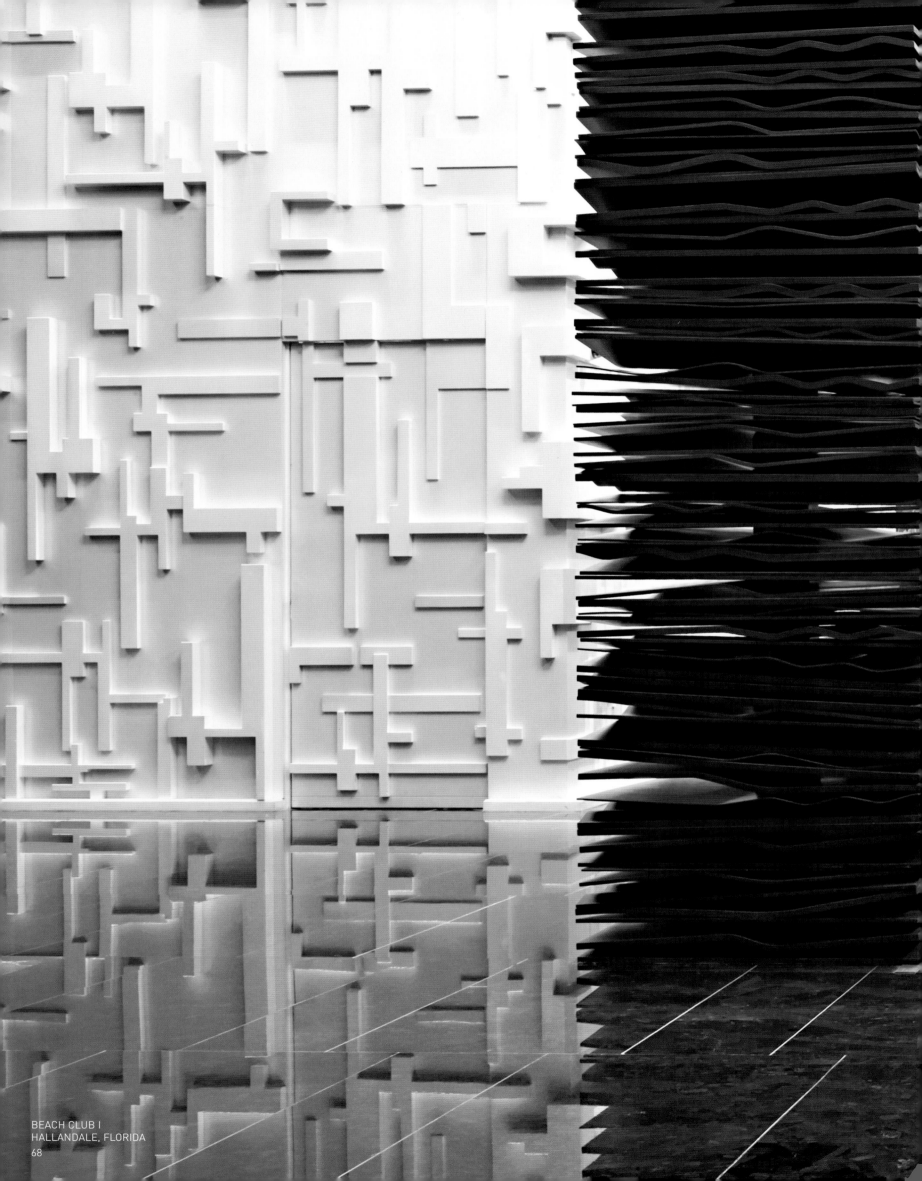

BEACH CLUB I
HALLANDALE, FLORIDA

CONCIERGE

GRAVES 601 HOTEL
MINNEAPOLIS

FOUR SEASONS HOTEL TOKYO AT MARUNOUCHI
TOKYO

TIFFANY & CO.
NEW YORK

LOTTE
BUSAN, KOREA

84

LOTTE
BUSAN, KOREA

EXCLUSIVITY

What is the difference between exclusivity and snobbery? Aren't they two words for the same thing? Then why does "exclusivity" sound alluring, beguiling, transporting and mysterious, and "snobbery" static, or just plain cruel?

Snobbery seeks to exclude people, whereas exclusivity rarifies and uplifts. Think of couture as a made-to-order approach that needn't always signify great expense, distinguishing a private refuge in a public space, perhaps, or special attention to details, a personal touch, an exceptional service. "Nothing typical," George and Glenn say, laughing when I ask them to define the difference.

"In any creative process, you have to ask yourself, 'How do I create and then create again and again something that is always extra-special, that offers a unique perspective to our client and his or her customer?' " says Glenn.

We see examples of snobbery all over: on the television, magazines, the web (expressed in the scolding, superior-sounding language of snark). Snobbery is a quick delineator in this age of babble disguised as revelation and information. Who is who? Who can we trust? What is quality? What is con? Snark and disdain create hierarchy, and hierarchy promises order, a social vortex in the center of space.

Many people are snobbish; for example, all the talking heads on the television news, whether they realize it or not. But few, if any, in the celebrity firmament are exclusive, insofar as it means quiet, not flashy, quality. Fashion designers, interior designers, decorators, chefs, athletes, socialites ... the last cultural example of anyone or anything exclusive I can think of was Jacqueline Kennedy Onassis, who, like Garbo, could be seen but never heard. Descriptions of Jackie in countless biographies always made her exclusivity palpable, like this passage from one that describes a few, pre-Aristotle Onassis winter days in 1966:

"After Gstaad, Jackie went to Rome and, despite assurances to friends that she wanted to spend 'a quiet few days,' the Roman aristocracy went into high gear. Everywhere she went, the adoring crowds cheered and applauded her. Princess Irene Galitzine threw a small dinner in her behalf and made her an ankle-length black gown for her return visit with the Pope. She dined with sculptor Pericle Fazzini at George's, a smart English restaurant. She went on a fox-hunt with her husband's former schoolmate, Count Dino Pecci-Blunt, and was entertained by Prince Aspreno Colonna at an elegant private dinner party for thirty at the 15th-century ocher-colored Palazzo Colonna. She also visited the villa of Gianni Agnelli at the exclusive beach resort of Forte dei Marmi."

Très chic, non?

Not only is exclusivity that something special you create—quality hiding in the details, a symphony of design elements waiting in quietude—it is those things, those plans, that person, that place, that love, which never "divulge everything at once," says Glenn.

Something exclusive is not necessarily something hidden, but something that keeps its secrets until they are discovered over time—like Jackie's view of the Mediterranean from Gianni Agnelli's: the more she looked, the more she no doubt saw. But Jackie being Jackie, very exclusive, never said a word—at least not for public consumption.

W HOTEL TIMES SQUARE
NEW YORK

DISCRIMINATING EDITS

Their professional spaces, their personal sanctuaries: The world according to George and Glenn is not arbitrarily arranged. Perhaps this great adventure called life, with all its many layers, cannot be controlled—but it can be edited.

On a cold winter's day, sunlight wraps their downtown Manhattan apartment, suspended over the Hudson River, like a transparent, shimmering cocoon. A visit with the dynamic duo finds their rigor and passion for their work illuminated and alive. A restrained, refined luxury permeates the place, but emotion and enthusiasm transcend any suggestion of the puritanically minimal. There's a joyous celebration of the details, from the nuts and bolts of the kitchen lighting to the walls inside a closet. George and Glenn can tell you how everything was made, where it was sourced, how it was put through a series of tests before it was deemed complete and then installed. Everything has a story; nothing is arbitrary.

"When you get out of design school," Glenn remembers, "your first temptation is to throw everything you can think of at the wall. But as you develop, you realize that the most important thing is not only to get your ideas out, but to pull them back, keeping only the most important elements and getting rid of everything else."

Duly noted. Home is where the details are, and the heart will surely follow. Among the details in their Greenwich Village residence: a three-legged chair by the Canadian designer Klaus Nienkamper, which took them a decade to acquire; an old laurel log from the bottom of a waterway in India, reclaimed for use as cabinetry and walls; an Anish Kapoor sculpture—

art and furniture emulate each other. Details, details, details … not just any travertine slabs shipped to New York, but only those laid out first like a giant jigsaw puzzle in the stonecutter's warehouse in Italy, supervised by a standard-bearing Yabu Pushelberg employee.

"In extraordinary spaces like the ones we are privileged to work in around the world, you have to be a strong editor as much as a strong designer," George says. "Too often design is bombastic, to please the client, but then it ends up dating in just a few years."

Design splendor lies in giving the eye time to see. It is in not having to claim every bit of space, but allowing one to "just be there," to breathe, look, personalize the experience, be drawn to objects, lighting, mood.

"Juxtapositions that exalt a piece of art and furniture, or playing opposites with the most selective technological material against something organic to attract—that is enough to create a strong and direct message that is almost simple because of its complexity," says Glenn.

When space and form are equal partners, the dance begins. Sight becomes vision, and what you see is as important as what you do not see (a lot like life).

With so many great commissions already, I wondered what was left for George and Glenn. Any dream job? "Doing a museum and an art gallery," Glenn answers. "The rigorous sense of ourselves as the designers, but also the necessary amounts of restraint needed to reassert the importance of the art and each artist's work, would be a thrilling challenge."

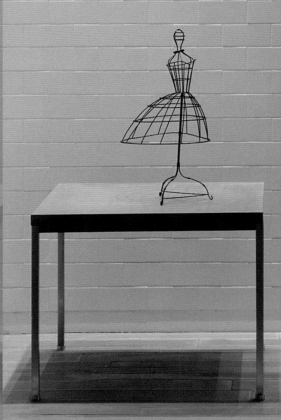

PIAZZA SEMPIONE
NEW YORK
140

BEACH CLUB II
HALLANDALE, FLORIDA

142

PRIVATE RESIDENCE
NEW YORK
144

LAS OLAS BEACH CLUB
FT. LAUDERDALE, FLORIDA

LOTTE
BUSAN, KOREA
166

LAS OLAS BEACH CLUB
FT. LAUDERDALE, FLORIDA

LANE CRAWFORD
BEIJING
186

THEATRICALITY & CEREMONY

How do you make something special? This is one of the first questions George and Glenn ask themselves, both philosophically and specifically, when they begin their design process.

An essential component in the answer is the dance of theatricality and ceremony, sparked by a well-designed space every time it is entered—never boring, and never so familiar that enchantment fades. Good design is not inert; it is a stage, a plot, motion, and mood, or a series of moods, unfolding, from front door to your room, from coat check to your table, from denim on display to beauty under glass. Is it a march, a sashay, a full gallop to the... library, kitchen, bedroom, or whichever is your favorite space?

The conversation turns to stairs.

"The meaning of stairs," George explains, "not only the physical things but the *seduction* of stairs... is very romantic."

"They're beautiful," Glenn adds. "The rise-to-run formula."

"A comfortable journey," George smiles. "The rise not too high, a generous amount of run so your whole foot is planted comfortably on the steps... "

Glenn continues, "It all becomes very effortless, and without realizing it, 'I'm upstairs already.' "

The stairs up the Statue of Liberty, tedious. The stairs at Versailles—as in the scene in Sofia Coppola's "Marie Antoinette" when the queen returns on a sunny day after an idyll at the Petite Trianon—not easy. Glenn and George's stairs at Carolina Herrera's boutique? Effortless drama. When I look up I always expect to see Gene Tierney from "Laura" coming down.

Consider the outdoor staircase at director George Cukor's house in Los Angeles, as described by Katharine Hepburn in her memoir, "Me." Elegant descending or ascending, emerging on the terrace, which was really the main floor, because the house was built on the side of a hill. The stairs added even more glamour to glamorous evenings, exits and entrances, theatricality and ceremony realized in the rituals of a sophisticated social life.

Hepburn describes dinners in candlelit rooms: "We all looked delicious." And the huge sofa Mr. Cukor had built in his famous, leather-walled Oval Room, where Hepburn would repair with the likes of Gregory Peck, Edith Sitwell, Somerset Maugham, Judy Garland, Laurence Olivier. One night, sitting between Groucho Marx and Igor Stravinsky, she wanted to talk to the latter about his experience with the lyrebirds in Australia, but Groucho kept interrupting.

"Poor Groucho, he wanted to talk, and I wanted to hear Stravinsky, who wanted to hear the lyrebirds, and they chose not to sing. Life life!" Hepburn recalls.

Conclusion? Life is the rise-to-run formula, like show biz, like stairs—what goes up also comes down, theatrically, ceremoniously, always in other places, other rooms.

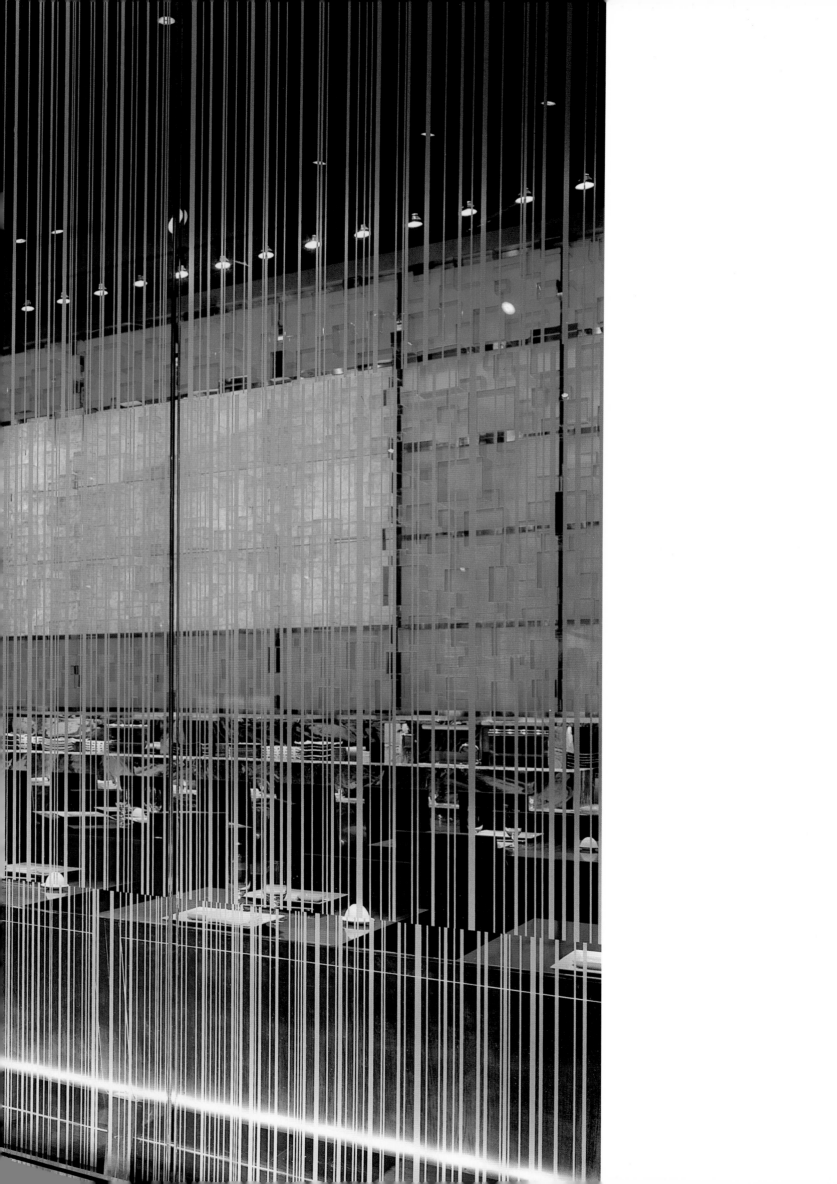

CAROLINA HERRERA
NEW YORK

LOTTE
BUSAN, KOREA

LOTTE
BUSAN, KOREA

LANE CRAWFORD
BEIJING
232

AMOREPACIFIC
114 Spring Street, New York
Completed: 2003
Photographer: David Joseph
*Korean skincare company Amorepacific opened
its first North American location in a historic building
in New York's SoHo district. The 3,000-square-foot
boutique incorporates interactive product displays,
two treatment rooms, and multiple sculpture
installations.*
Pages 66, 110

THE AMORE STAR
50-17 Myong-Dong 2-GA, Jung-Gu, Seoul
Completed: 2005
Photographer: Nacasa & Partners Inc.
*The Amore Star is a four-story concept store in
Seoul's Myong-Dong neighborhood, which caters
to a young, fashionable crowd. The store showcases
the Pacific Corporation's Laneige line of cosmetics,
along with treatment rooms, a teaching studio,
and a cafe.*
Page 78

BEACH CLUB I
1850 South Ocean Drive, Hallandale, Florida
Completed: 2006
Photographer: Evan Dion
*The towers of the Beach Club, a luxury condominium
complex situated between Miami and Ft. Lauderdale,
have two-story lobbies with opposing color schemes.
Beach Club I's lobby is rendered in cool blues and
browns.*
Page 68

BEACH CLUB II
1830 South Ocean Drive, Hallandale, Florida
Completed: 2006
Photographer: Evan Dion
*The lobby of Beach Club II features a warm
palette meant to evoke sand and beach.*
Page 142

BERGDORF GOODMAN
754 Fifth Avenue, New York
Completed: 1999
Photographer: David Joseph
*The cosmetics department at luxury retailer
Bergdorf Goodman, located in the former Cornelius
Vanderbilt mansion, occupies a 15,560-square-foot
space in the basement level. The jewelry department
on the ground floor encompasses
4,370 square feet.*
Pages 14, 48, 174

BLUE FIN
1567 Broadway, New York
Completed: 2002
Photographer: Evan Dion
*Located at the W Hotel Times Square, this 400-seat
restaurant features a sushi bar and café-style seat-
ing on the ground floor, with a main dining room
and three private spaces upstairs.*
Page 96

BYMARK
66 Wellington Street West, Toronto
Completed: 2002
Photographer: Evan Dion
*Bymark is situated on two floors at Mies van der
Rohe's TD Centre in Toronto's financial district.
The 7,500-square-foot restaurant features a main
dining area, three private rooms that seat up to
14 guests each, and a bar/lounge within an atrium.*
Pages 88, 150

CAROLINA HERRERA
954 Madison Avenue, New York
Completed: 2000
Photographer: David Joseph
*The North American flagship of clothing designer
Carolina Herrera is housed in the landmarked
Hubert de Givenchy building. The store covers
3,000 square feet on three floors.*
Pages 116, 208

PRIVATE RESIDENCE
Miami
Completed: 1999
Photographer: Ron Baxter Smith
A 2,500-square-foot bungalow from the 1950s was renovated to create an airy, minimalist space.
Pages 44, 154

PRIVATE RESIDENCE
New York
Completed: 2007
Photographer: Evan Dion
This 3,800-square-foot Greenwich Village home is in a Richard Meier-designed tower overlooking the Hudson River.
Pages 24, 34, 62, 120, 144, 158, 224

PRIVATE RESIDENCE
Toronto
Completed: 2001
Photographer: Ron Baxter Smith
A 3,500-square-foot Georgian structure from the 1960s was gutted to create this home in the Bennington Heights neighborhood.
Pages 138, 162, 168

SHIBUYA
3799 Las Vegas Boulevard South, Las Vegas
Completed: 2004
Photographer: David Joseph
Shibuya, named for Tokyo's frenetic center of fashion and nightlife, is located in the MGM Grand Hotel & Casino. The 7,000-square-foot space comprises three dining areas: a 50-foot marble sushi bar; the main room, inspired by a bento box; and a grill room with communal dining.
Pages 12, 92, 188, 212

SMYTH
85 West Broadway, New York
Completed: 2009
Photographer: Evan Dion
Smyth, part of the Thompson Hotels group, is located in a 13-floor building in Tribeca.
Pages 20, 50, 164, 206, 216

ST. REGIS HOTEL SAN FRANCISCO
125 Third Street, San Francisco
Completed: 2005
Photographer: Joe Fletcher Photography, except Dennis Anderson, page 106
Situated in a 40-story building next to the San Francisco Museum of Modern Art, the St. Regis comprises 260 hotel rooms and suites, ranging from 450 to 3,200 square feet. The facility offers a 9,000-square-foot spa; 95-seat fine dining restaurant Ame; 74-seat breakfast restaurant Vitrine; and a lobby bar featuring a contemporary interpretation of the famed mural at the King Cole bar at the St. Regis New York.
Pages 26, 86, 106

TIFFANY & CO.
37 Wall Street, New York
Completed: 2007
Photographer: Evan Dion
This contemporary boutique occupies the ground floor and mezzanine of a 25-story historic Beaux-Arts building in downtown Manhattan. The main selling area of the 11,000-square-foot store is divided into numerous translucent salons.
Pages 38, 52, 76, 126, 152, 190, 226

W HOTEL TIMES SQUARE
1567 Broadway, New York
Completed: 2001
Photographer: Evan Dion
This 57-floor, 509-room hotel features a 6,000-square-foot lobby and bar/seating area on the seventh floor, Blue Fin restaurant, and Rande Gerber's bar/screening room The Whiskey.
Pages 36, 128, 136

ACKNOWLEDGEMENTS

We'd like to thank those who have influenced our world. Many inspired us in a direct way through our work—they might not have realized it, but they informed us of a new way of thinking and looking. Others helped us less tangibly, but no less in importance. They guided and navigated us through the challenges of developing a vibrant and productive design studio. Collectively, they—along with our families, both given and chosen—saw possibilities before we did.

A note of thanks also goes to our colleague Tara Browne, whose critical eye and unyielding energy, travelling around the world to every location, were essential in the creation of this book. Her travelling companion, photographer Evan Dion, must not be overlooked; we thank his focus in capturing the essence of our work. For their enthusiasm and professionalism, thanks must also go to author William Norwich, publisher Anthony Iannacci, and editor Carolyn Horwitz for making this, our first monograph, happen.

Special thanks go to: Cindy Allen, Steven Aronoff, Irene Bell, Bonnie Brooks, Daniel Chuao, Anthony Davy, Scott Eunson, Pascale Girardin, Lee Hodges, Lillian Hsu, Kieran Keaveney, Charles Khabouth, Edward Lam, Dennis Lin, Marc Littlejohn, Joanne McLaughlin, Phillip Moody, Deborah Moss, Christine Nakaoka, Gino Panarese, Helen Poon, Christine Ralphs, Joel Rath, Mayer Rus, Hirotoshi Sawada, Isadore Sharp, Jennifer Woo, Tomoko Yabu, and Jessie Yoshida.